The "I Am" Book

(because of Jesus Christ, I am)

By

Dale E. Vick

© Copyright 2008, Dale Edward Vick

All Rights Reserved.

No part of this book may be reproduced, stored in a
retrieval system, or transmitted by any means,
electronic, mechanical, photocopying, recording,
or otherwise, without written permission
from the author.

ISBN: 978-0-615-26325-0

All Scripture quotations are taken from the *King James Version*.

Note to the Reader

Let me encourage you to meditate on the scripture under each heading as an individual thought.

Over the course of a few minutes, hours and days you will begin to see the depth of what the Lord Jesus Christ did for you and how it applies to your daily life.

God encourages us to walk in the Word. As you meditate in the Word it will become part of you.

Who God is will begin to rise up and meet your daily experiences with a fresh new mindset. The Bible will give you a new way of looking at old problems you have yet to overcome.

Remember: Greater is he that is in you than he that is in the world!

My prayer for you is that you will fall deeper in love with the One who gave himself for our sins and is now set down on the right hand of the Father making intercession for us.

There is space for you to make notes after each thought. Let me encourage you to write down those thoughts. I have found over the years that the things I write down will be the things that remain fresh in me.

May you grow in grace and in the knowledge of our Lord Jesus Christ!

Dale E. Vick

Youngsville, NC

www.HeistheRock.org

*I have listed **one hundred and seventy two** privileges that we **<u>have and are</u>** because of the death, burial and resurrection of the Lord Jesus Christ.*

May their reality find lodging in your heart as you strive to walk with Him whom to know is to have everlasting life!

Table of Contents

Love 1

Life 2

Identity 11

Security 15

Gift 17

Deliverance 19

Hope 27

Growth 35

Direction 46

Victory 57

Death 66

Virgil said,

Death twitches my ear. Live, he says, I am coming.

Jesus said,

"But is now made manifest by the appearing of our Saviour Jesus Christ, who hath <u>abolished death</u>, and hath brought life and immortality to light through the gospel:"

Love

I am loved!

"For God so loved the world, that he gave his only begotten Son, that whosoever believeth in him should not perish, but have everlasting life." John 3:16

"Behold, what manner of love the Father hath bestowed upon us, that we should be called the sons of God: therefore the world knoweth us not, because it knew him not. Beloved, now are we the sons of God, and it doth not yet appear what we shall be: but we know that, when he shall appear, we shall be like him; for we shall see him as he is." I John 3:1, 2

I am loved unconditionally!

"As the Father hath loved me, so have I loved you: continue ye in my love." John 15:9

I am walking in love!

"Be ye therefore followers of God, as dear children; and walk in love, as Christ also hath loved us, and hath given himself for us an offering and a sacrifice to God for a sweet-smelling savour." Ephesians 5:1, 2

Life

I am alive because of Christ!

"And if Christ be in you, the body is dead because of sin; but the Spirit is life because of righteousness." Romans 8:10

I am fearfully and wonderfully made!

"I will praise thee; for I am fearfully and wonderfully made: marvellous are thy works; and that my soul knoweth right well." Psalm 139:14

I am in the world!

"And now I am no more in the world, but these are in the world, and I come to thee. Holy Father, keep through thine own name those whom thou hast given me, that they may be one, as we are." John 17:11

I am in God's book!

"Thine eyes did see my substance, yet being unperfect; and in thy book all my members were written, which in continuance were fashioned, when as yet there was none of them." Psalm 139:16

"And I intreat thee also, true yokefellow, help those women which laboured with me in the gospel, with Clement also, and with other my fellowlabourers, whose names are in the book of life." Philippians 4:3

I am free to enter His presence at any time!

"Let us therefore come boldly unto the throne of grace, that we may obtain mercy, and find grace to help in time of need." Hebrews 4:16

I am a member of His body, flesh, and bones!

"That he might sanctify and cleanse it with the washing of water by the word, That he might present it to himself a glorious church, not having spot, or wrinkle, or any such thing; but that it should be holy and without blemish. For we are members of his body, of his flesh, and of his bones." Ephesians 5:26, 27, 30

I am as He is!

"Herein is our love made perfect, that we may have boldness in the day of judgment: because as he is, so are we in this world." I John 4:17

I am groaning for home!

"For in this we groan, earnestly desiring to be clothed upon with our house which is from heaven: If so be that being clothed we shall not be found naked. For we that are in this tabernacle do groan, being burdened: not for that we would be unclothed, but clothed upon, that mortality might be swallowed up of life." II Corinthians 5:2-4

I am redeemed by His Blood!

"Neither by the blood of goats and calves, but by his own blood he entered in once into the holy place, having obtained eternal redemption for us." Hebrews 9:12

I am free!

"For the law of the Spirit of life in Christ Jesus hath made me free from the law of sin and death." Romans 8:2

"For he that is called in the Lord, being a servant, is the Lord's freeman: likewise also he that is called, being free, is Christ's servant." I Corinthians 7:22

"Stand fast therefore in the liberty wherewith Christ hath made us free, and be not entangled again with the yoke of bondage." Galatians 5:1

I am thankful!

"And let the peace of God rule in your hearts, to the which also ye are called in one body; and be ye thankful." Colossians 3:15

"Enter into his gates with thanksgiving, and into his courts with praise: be thankful unto him, and bless his name." Psalm 100:4

I am walking in Christ!

"Therefore we are buried with him by baptism into death: that like as Christ was raised up from the dead by the glory of the Father, even so we also should walk in newness of life." Romans 6:4

"There is therefore now no condemnation to them which are in Christ Jesus, who walk not after the flesh, but after the Spirit." Romans 8:1

"(For we walk by faith, not by sight:)" II Corinthians 5; 7

"And what agreement hath the temple of God with idols? for ye are the temple of the living God; as God hath said, I will dwell in them, and walk in them; and I will be their God, and they shall be my people." II Corinthians 6:16

"If we live in the Spirit, let us also walk in the Spirit." Galatians 5:25

I am quickened!

"And you hath he quickened, who were dead in trespasses and sins;" Ephesians 2:1

"Even when we were dead in sins, hath quickened us together with Christ, (by grace ye are saved ;)" Ephesians 2:5

I am circumcised in Him!

"In whom also ye are circumcised with the circumcision made without hands, in putting off the body of the sins of the flesh by the circumcision of Christ:" Colossians 2:11

I am for God because God is for me!

"What shall we then say to these things? If God be for us, who can be against us?" Romans 8:31

I am near to God!

"Let us draw near with a true heart in full assurance of faith, having our hearts sprinkled from an evil conscience, and our bodies washed with pure water." Hebrews 10:22

I am the Temple of God!

"Know ye not that ye are the temple of God, and that the Spirit of God dwelleth in you?" I Corinthians 3:16

"What? Know ye not that your body is the temple of the Holy Ghost which is in you, which ye have of God, and ye are not your own? For ye are bought with a price: therefore glorify God in your body, and in your spirit, which are God's."

I Corinthians 6:19, 20

I am married to Christ Jesus the Lord!

"Wherefore, my brethren, ye also are become dead to the law by the body of Christ; that ye should be married to another, even to him who is raised from the dead, that we should bring forth fruit unto God." Romans 7:4

I am Holy!

"Because it is written, Be ye holy; for I am holy. And if ye call on the Father, who without respect of persons judgeth according to every man's work, pass the time of your sojourning here in fear: Forasmuch as ye know that ye were not redeemed with corruptible things, as silver and gold, from your vain conversation received by tradition from your fathers; But with the precious blood of Christ, as of a lamb without blemish and without spot: Who verily was foreordained before the foundation of the world, but was manifest in these last times for you, Who by him do believe in God, that raised him up from the dead, and gave him glory; that your faith and hope might be in God. Seeing ye have purified your souls in obeying the truth through the Spirit unto unfeigned love of the brethren, see that ye love one another with a pure heart fervently: "

I Peter 1:16-22

I am not of the world!

"They are not of the world, even as I am not of the world." John 17:16

"If ye were of the world, the world would love his own: but because ye are not of the world, but I have chosen you out of the world, therefore the world hateth you."

John 15:19

I am a sweet fragrance to my Father!

"Now thanks be unto God, which always causeth us to triumph in Christ, and maketh manifest the savour of his knowledge by us in every place." II Corinthians 2:14

I am God's building!

"For we are labourers together with God: ye are God's husbandry, ye are God's building." I Corinthians 3:9

Identity

I am God's husbandry!

"For we are labourers together with God: ye are God's husbandry, ye are God's building." I Corinthians 3:9

I am in the image of His Son!

"For whom he did foreknow, he also did predestinate to be conformed to the image of his Son, that he might be the firstborn among many brethren." Romans 8:29

I am joined to the Lord!

"But he that is joined unto the Lord is one spirit." I Corinthians 6:17

I am made perfect in one!

"I in them, and thou in me, that they may be made perfect in one; and that the world may know that thou hast sent me, and hast loved them, as thou hast loved me."

John 17:23

I am adopted!

"Having predestinated us unto the adoption of children by Jesus Christ to himself, according to the good pleasure of his will," Ephesians 1:5

I am chosen!

"Ye have not chosen me, but I have chosen you, and ordained you, that ye should go and bring forth fruit, and that your fruit should remain: that whatsoever ye shall ask of the Father in my name, he may give it you." John 15:16

"But we are bound to give thanks alway to God for you, brethren beloved of the Lord, because God hath from the beginning chosen you to salvation through sanctification of the Spirit and belief of the truth:" II Thessalonians 2:13

I am joint-heirs with Christ Jesus!

"The Spirit itself beareth witness with our spirit, that we are the children of God: And if children, then heirs; heirs of God, and joint-heirs with Christ; if so be that we suffer with him, that we may be also glorified together." Romans 8:16, 17

I am seated in the throne with Him!

"Looking unto Jesus the author and finisher of our faith; who for the joy that was set before him endured the cross, despising the shame, and is set down at the right hand of the throne of God." Hebrews 12:2

"To whom God would make known what is the riches of the glory of this mystery among the Gentiles; which is Christ in you, the hope of glory:" Colossians 1:27

Dale E. Vick

I am nigh!

"Much more then, being now justified by his blood, we shall be saved from wrath through him." Romans 5:9

"Wherefore remember, that ye being in time past Gentiles in the flesh, who are called Uncircumcision by that which is called the Circumcision in the flesh made by hands; That at that time ye were without Christ, being aliens from the commonwealth of Israel, and strangers from the covenants of promise, having no hope, and without God in the world: But now in Christ Jesus ye who sometimes were far off are made nigh by the blood of Christ." Ephesians 2; 11-13

Security

I am safe in His hands!

"And I give unto them eternal life; and they shall never perish, neither shall any man pluck them out of my hand." John 10:28

"And this is life eternal, that they might know thee the only true God, and Jesus Christ, whom thou hast sent." John 17:3

I am engraved on the palms of His hands!

"Behold, I have graven thee upon the palms of my hands;" Isaiah 49:16

I am preserved!

"And the very God of peace sanctify you wholly; and I pray God your whole spirit and soul and body be preserved blameless unto the coming of our Lord Jesus Christ."

I Thessalonians 5:23

"Jude, the servant of Jesus Christ, and brother of James, to them that are sanctified by God the Father, and preserved in Jesus Christ, and called:" Jude 1

I am persuaded!

"For I am persuaded, that neither death, nor life, nor angels, nor principalities, nor powers, nor things present, nor things to come, Nor height nor depth, nor any other creature, shall be able to separate us from the love of God, which is in Christ Jesus our Lord." Romans 8:38, 39

I am confirmed!

"Who shall also confirm you unto the end, that ye may be blameless in the day of our Lord Jesus Christ." I Corinthians 1:8

Gift

I am rich!

"For ye know the grace of our Lord Jesus Christ, that, though he was rich, yet for your sakes he became poor, that ye through his poverty might be rich." II Corinthians 8:9

"Being enriched in every thing to all bountifulness, which causeth through us thanksgiving to God." II Corinthians 9:11

I am God's gift to His Son!

"Ask of me, and I shall give thee the heathen for thine inheritance, and the uttermost parts of the earth for thy possession." Psalm 2:8

I am calling for my Father!

"For ye have not received the spirit of bondage again to fear; but ye have received the Spirit of adoption, whereby we cry, Abba, Father." Romans 8:15

Dale E. Vick

I am heir of the world!

"For the promise, that he should be the heir of the world, was not to Abraham, or to his seed, through the law, but through the righteousness of faith." Romans 4:13

Deliverance

I am delivered from corruption!

"Whereby are given unto us exceeding great and precious promises: that by these ye might be partakers of the divine nature, having escaped the corruption that is in the world through lust." II Peter 1:4

I am delivered from judgment!

"Therefore as by the offence of one judgment came upon all men to condemnation; even so by the righteousness of one the free gift came upon all men unto justification of life." Romans 5:18

I am delivered from the power of sin!

"Whom God hath set forth to be a propitiation through faith in his blood, to declare his righteousness for the remission of sins that are past, through the forbearance of God;" Romans 3:25

I am delivered from an unsound mind!

"For God hath not given us the spirit of fear; but of power, and of love, and of a sound mind." II Timothy 1:7

I am delivered from the power of darkness!

"Who hath delivered us from the power of darkness, and hath translated us into the kingdom of his dear Son:" Colossians 1:13

I am dead to sin!

"God forbid. How shall we, that are dead to sin, live any longer therein? Likewise reckon ye also yourselves to be dead indeed unto sin, but alive unto God through Jesus Christ our Lord." Romans 6:2, 11

I am safe under His wings!

"He shall cover thee with his feathers, and under his wings shalt thou trust: his truth shall be thy shield and buckler." Psalm 91:4

I am released from my sin by His Blood!

"And, having made peace through the blood of his cross, by him to reconcile all things unto himself; by him, I say, whether they be things in earth, or things in heaven." Colossians 1:20

I am equipped with the Sword of the Spirit!

"For the word of God is quick, and powerful, and sharper than any twoedged sword, piercing even to the dividing asunder of soul and spirit, and of the joints and marrow, and is a discerner of the thoughts and intents of the heart." Hebrews 4:12

"And take the helmet of salvation, and the sword of the Spirit, which is the word of God:" Ephesians 6:17

Dale E. Vick

I am at peace by the Blood of His Cross!

"For he is our peace, who hath made both one, and hath broken down the middle wall of partition between us;" Ephesians 2:14

I am working according to His working in me!

"For this cause also thank we God without ceasing, because, when ye received the word of God which ye heard of us, ye received it not as the word of men, but as it is in truth, the word of God, which effectually worketh also in you that believe."

I Thessalonians 2:13

"And what is the exceeding greatness of his power to us-ward who believe, according to the working of his mighty power," Ephesians 1:19

"Now unto him that is able to do exceeding abundantly above all that we ask or think, according to the power that worketh in us," Ephesians 3:20

I am not condemned!

"Who is he that condemneth? It is Christ that died, yea rather, that is risen again, who is even at the right hand of God, who also maketh intercession for us." Romans 8:34

I am reconciled by the cross!

"For he is our peace, who hath made both one, and hath broken down the middle wall of partition between us; Having abolished in his flesh the enmity, even the law of commandments contained in ordinances; for to make in himself of twain one new man, so making peace; And that he might reconcile both unto God in one body by the cross, having slain the enmity thereby: And came and preached peace to you which were afar off, and to them that were nigh. For through him we both have access by one Spirit unto the Father." Ephesians 2:14-18

I am bought with a price!

"Ye are bought with a price; be not ye the servants of men." I Corinthians 7:23

I am blessed beyond the curse!

"Christ hath redeemed us from the curse of the law, being made a curse for us: for it is written, Cursed is every one that hangeth on a tree:" Galatians 3:13

I am not appointed to wrath!

"For God hath not appointed us to wrath, but to obtain salvation by our Lord Jesus Christ, Who died for us, that, whether we wake or sleep, we should live together with him." I Thessalonians 5:9

I am not entangled!

"Stand fast therefore in the liberty wherewith Christ hath made us free, and be not entangled again with the yoke of bondage." Galatians 5:1

I am casting down!

"(For the weapons of our warfare are not carnal, but mighty through God to the pulling down of strong holds;) Casting down imaginations, and every high thing that exalteth itself against the knowledge of God, and bringing into captivity every thought to the obedience of Christ;" II Corinthians 10: 4, 5

I am going out when He calls!

"Then we which are alive and remain shall be caught up together with them in the clouds, to meet the Lord in the air: and so shall we ever be with the Lord."

I Thessalonians 4:17

Hope

I am accepted in the beloved!

"To the praise of the glory of his grace, wherein he hath made us accepted in the beloved. In whom we have redemption through his blood, the forgiveness of sins, according to the riches of his grace; wherein he hath abounded toward us in all wisdom and prudence; Having made known unto us the mystery of his will, according to his good pleasure which he hath purposed in himself: That in the dispensation of the fulness of times he might gather together in one all things in Christ, both which are in heaven, and which are on earth; even in him: In whom also we have obtained an inheritance, being predestinated according to the purpose of him who worketh all things after the counsel of his own will: That we should be to the praise of his glory, who first trusted in Christ." Ephesians 1:6-12

I am seated in the heavens with Christ Jesus!

"Blessed be the God and Father of our Lord Jesus Christ, who hath blessed us with all spiritual blessings in heavenly places in Christ:" Ephesians 1:3

"And hath raised us up together, and made us sit together in heavenly places in Christ Jesus:" Ephesians 2:6

I am established!

"Rooted and built up in him, and stablished in the faith, as ye have been taught, abounding therein with thanksgiving." Colossians 2:7

I am named after Him!

"For this cause I bow my knees unto the Father of our Lord Jesus Christ, Of whom the whole family in heaven and earth is named," Ephesians 3:14, 15

I am complete in Him!

"And ye are complete in him, which is the head of all principality and power:"

Colossians 2; 10

I am not charged!

"Who shall lay any thing to the charge of God's elect? It is God that justifieth."

Romans 8:33

I am a new person in Christ!

"Therefore if any man be in Christ, he is a new creature: old things are passed away; behold, all things are become new." II Corinthians 5:17

"And that ye put on the new man, which after God is created in righteousness and true holiness." Ephesians 4:24

"Having abolished in his flesh the enmity, even the law of commandments contained in ordinances; for to make in himself of twain one new man, so making peace;"

Ephesians 2:15

I am of Him!

"For of him, and through him, and to him, are all things: to whom be glory for ever. Amen." Romans 11:36

I am a child of light!

"For ye were sometimes darkness, but now are ye light in the Lord: walk as children of light:" Ephesians 5:8

"Ye are all the children of light, and the children of the day: we are not of the night, nor of darkness." I Thessalonians 5:5

I am salt!

"Ye are the salt of the earth: but if the salt have lost his savour, wherewith shall it be salted? it is thenceforth good for nothing, but to be cast out, and to be trodden under foot of men." Matthew 5:13

I am a chosen generation!

"But ye are a chosen generation, a royal priesthood, an holy nation, a peculiar people; that ye should shew forth the praises of him who hath called you out of darkness into his marvellous light:" I Peter 2:9

I am not ashamed!

"For I am not ashamed of the gospel of Christ: for it is the power of God unto salvation to every one that believeth; to the Jew first, and also to the Greek." Romans 1:16

I am a city set on a hill!

"Ye are the light of the world. A city that is set on an hill cannot be hid." Matthew 5:14

I am enriched in speech and knowledge!

"That in every thing ye are enriched by him, in all utterance, and in all knowledge;"

I Corinthians 1:5

I am rooted and grounded in love!

"That Christ may dwell in your hearts by faith; that ye, being rooted and grounded in love, May be able to comprehend with all saints what is the breadth, and length, and depth, and height; And to know the love of Christ, which passeth knowledge, that ye might be filled with all the fulness of God." Ephesians 3:17-19

I am built upon the foundation!

"And are built upon the foundation of the apostles and prophets, Jesus Christ himself being the chief corner stone; In whom all the building fitly framed together groweth unto an holy temple in the Lord:" Ephesians 2:20,21

I am blessed with faithful Abraham!

"Know ye therefore that they which are of faith, the same are the children of Abraham. And the scripture, foreseeing that God would justify the heathen through faith, preached before the gospel unto Abraham, saying, In thee shall all nations be blessed. So then they which be of faith are blessed with faithful Abraham." Galatians 3:7-9

I am known of God!

"But now, after that ye have known God, or rather are known of God, how turn ye again to the weak and beggarly elements, whereunto ye desire again to be in bondage?" Galatians 4:9

I am more than a conqueror!

"Nay, in all these things we are more than conquerors through him that loved us." Romans 8:37

"Who shall separate us from the love of Christ? shall tribulation, or distress, or persecution, or famine, or nakedness, or peril, or sword? For I am persuaded, that neither death, nor life, nor angels, nor principalities, nor powers, nor things present, nor things to come, Nor height, nor depth, nor any other creature, shall be able to separate us from the love of God, which is in Christ Jesus our Lord."

Romans 8:35, 38, 39

I am looking at the eternal!

"For our light affliction, which is but for a moment, worketh for us a far more exceeding and eternal weight of glory; While we look not at the things which are seen, but at the things which are not seen: for the things which are seen are temporal; but the things which are not seen are eternal." II Corinthians 4:17, 18

I am trusting in His promise!

"In hope of eternal life, which God, that cannot lie, promised before the world began;" Titus 1:2

Growth

I am an able minister!

"Who also hath made us able ministers of the new testament; not of the letter, but of the spirit: for the letter killeth, but the spirit giveth life." II Corinthians 3:6

I am watching and standing!

"Watch ye, stand fast in the faith, quit you like men, be strong. Let all your things be done with charity." I Corinthians 16:13, 14

I am fully dressed for the fight!

"Finally, my brethren, be strong in the Lord, and in the power of his might. Put on the whole armour of God, that ye may be able to stand against the wiles of the devil. For we wrestle not against flesh and blood, but against principalities, against powers, against the rulers of the darkness of this world, against spiritual wickedness in high places. Wherefore take unto you the whole armour of God, that ye may be able to withstand in the evil day, and having done all, to stand. Stand therefore, having your loins girt about with truth, and having on the breastplate of righteousness; And your feet shod with the preparation of the gospel of peace; Above all, taking the shield of faith, wherewith ye shall be able to quench all the fiery darts of the wicked. And take the helmet of salvation, and the sword of the Spirit, which is the word of God: Praying always with all prayer and supplication in the Spirit, and watching thereunto with all perseverance and supplication for all saints;" Ephesians 6:10-18

I am what I am!

"But by the grace of God I am what I am: and his grace which was bestowed upon me was not in vain;" I Corinthians 15:10

I am unblameable!

"And you, that were sometime alienated and enemies in your mind by wicked works, yet now hath he reconciled In the body of his flesh through death, to present you holy and unblameable and unreproveable in his sight:" Colossians 1:21, 22

I am content!

"Not that I speak in respect of want: for I have learned, in whatsoever state I am, therewith to be content." Philippians 4:11

I am instructed!

"I know both how to be abased, and I know how to abound: every where and in all things I am instructed both to be full and to be hungry, both to abound and to suffer need." Philippians 4:12

I am being transformed!

"And be not conformed to this world: but be ye transformed by the renewing of your mind, that ye may prove what is that good, and acceptable, and perfect, will of God." Romans 12:2

I am united with Jesus in his death, burial and resurrection!

"Know ye not, that so many of us as were baptized into Jesus Christ were baptized into his death? Therefore we are buried with him by baptism into death: that like as Christ was raised up from the dead by the glory of the Father, even so we also should walk in newness of life:" Romans 6:3, 4

I am overcoming the accuser by the Blood of the Lamb!

"And I heard a loud voice saying in heaven, Now is come salvation, and strength, and the kingdom of our God, and the power of his Christ: for the accuser of our brethren is cast down, which accused them before our God day and night. And they overcame him by the blood of the Lamb, and by the word of their testimony; and they loved not their lives unto the death." Revelation 12:10, 11

"Ye are of God, little children, and have overcome them: because greater is he that is in you, than he that is in the world." I John 4:4

"These things I have spoken unto you, that in me ye might have peace. In the world ye shall have tribulation: but be of good cheer; I have overcome the world." John 16:33

I am risen!

"Buried with him in baptism, wherein also ye are risen with him through the faith of the operation of God, who hath raised him from the dead." Colossians 2:12

"If ye then be risen with Christ, seek those things which are above, where Christ sitteth on the right hand of God." Colossians 3:1

I am laboring!

"Whereunto I also labour, striving according to his working, which worketh in me mightily." Colossians 1:29

I am filled with the fruits of righteousness!

"Being filled with the fruits of righteousness, which are by Jesus Christ, unto the glory and praise of God." Philippians 1:11

I am following after!

"Not as though I had already attained, either were already perfect: but I follow after, if that I may apprehend that for which also I am apprehended of Christ Jesus."

Philippians 3:12

I am the recipient of His Word!

"For I have given unto them the words which thou gavest me; and they have received them, and have known surely that I came out from thee, and they have believed that thou didst sent me." John 17:8

I am His personal creation!

"And to make all men see what is the fellowship of the mystery, which from the beginning of the world hath been hid in God, who created all things by Jesus Christ:" Ephesians 3:9

"For by him were all things created, that are in heaven, and that are in earth, visible and invisible, whether they be thrones, or dominions, or principalities, or powers: all things were created by him, and for him:" Colossians 1:16

"And have put on the new man, which is renewed in knowledge after the image of him that created him:" Colossians 3:10

I am the righteousness of God!

"For he hath made him to be sin for us, who knew no sin; that we might be made the righteousness of God in him." II Corinthians 5:21

I am a possessor!

"But of him are ye in Christ Jesus, who of God is made unto us wisdom, and righteousness, and sanctification, and redemption:" I Corinthians 1:30

I am changed from glory to glory!

"But we all, with open face beholding as in a glass the glory of the Lord, are changed into the same image from glory to glory, even as by the Spirit of the Lord."

II Corinthians 3:18

I am confident!

"In whom we have boldness and access with confidence by the faith of him."

Ephesians 3:12

I am the elect of God!

"Who shall lay any thing to the charge of God's elect? It is God that justifieth."

Romans 8:33

"Put on therefore, as the elect of God, holy and beloved, bowels of mercies, kindness, humbleness of mind, meekness, longsuffering;" Colossians 3:13

"Elect according to the fore-knowledge of God the Father, through sanctification of the Spirit, unto obedience and sprinkling of the blood of Jesus Christ: Grace unto you, and peace, be multiplied." I Peter 1:2

I am helped!

"The Lord is my strength and my shield; my heart trusted in him, and I am helped: therefore my heart greatly rejoiceth; and with my song will I praise him." Psalm 28:7

I am apprehended!

"Brethren, I count not myself to have apprehended: but this one thing I do, forgetting those things which are behind, and reaching forth unto those things which are before, I press toward the mark for the prize of the high calling of God in Christ Jesus." Philippians 3:13, 14

I am justified by grace!

"Knowing that a man is not justified by the works of the law, but by the faith of Jesus Christ, even we have believed in Jesus Christ, that we might be justified by the faith of Christ, and not by the works of the law: for by the works of the law shall no flesh be justified." Galatians 2:16

I am to His praise!

"That we should be to the praise of his glory, who first trusted in Christ." Ephesians 1:12

I am troubled!

"We are troubled on every side, yet not distressed; we are perplexed, but not in despair; Persecuted, but not forsaken; cast down, but not destroyed; Always bearing about in the body the dying of the Lord Jesus, that the life also of Jesus might be made manifest in our body. For we which live are alway delivered unto death for Jesus' sake, that the life also of Jesus might be made manifest in our mortal flesh." II Corinthians 4:8-11

I am blameless and harmless!

"That ye may be blameless and harmless, the sons of God, without rebuke, in the midst of a crooked and perverse nation, among whom ye shine as lights in the world;"

Philippians 2:15

I am led by the Spirit of God!

"For as many as are led by the Spirit of God, they are the sons of God." Romans 8:14

I am not terrified!

"And in nothing terrified by your adversaries: which is to them an evident token of perdition, but to you of salvation, and that of God." Philippians 1:28

Direction

I am an ambassador for Christ!

"Now then we are ambassadors for Christ, as though God did beseech you by us: we pray you in Christ's stead, be ye reconciled to God." II Corinthians 5:20

I am without offence!

"That ye may approve things that are excellent; that ye may be sincere and without offence till the day of Christ;" Philippians 1:10

I am set for the defense of the gospel!

"knowing that I am set for the defence of the gospel."

Philippians 1:17

I am ready!

"So, as much as in me is, I am ready to preach the gospel to you" Romans 1:15

I am the epistle of Christ!

"Forasmuch as ye are manifestly declared to be the epistle of Christ ministered by us, written not with ink, but with the Spirit of the living God; not in tables of stone, but in fleshy tables of the heart." II Corinthians 3:3

I am become weak for Christ's sake!

"To the weak became I as weak, that I might gain the weak: I am made all things to all men, that I might by all means save some." I Corinthians 9:22

Dale E. Vick

I am sent as Jesus was sent!

"As thou hast sent me into the world, even so have I also sent them into the world."

John 17:18

I am comforted so I can comfort!

"Blessed be God, even the Father of our Lord Jesus Christ, the Father of mercies, and the God of all comfort; Who comforteth us in all our tribulation, that we may be able to comfort them which are in any trouble, by the comfort wherewith we ourselves are comforted of God." II Corinthians 1:3, 4

I am fruitful!

"That ye might walk worthy of the Lord unto all pleasing, being fruitful in every good work, and increasing in the knowledge of God;" Colossians 1:10

"And not holding the Head, from which all the body by joints and bands having nourishment ministered, and knit together, increaseth with the increase of God." Colossians 2:19

I am forgiven so I can forgive!

"For if ye forgive men their trespasses, your heavenly Father will also forgive you:" Matthew 6:14

"If we confess our sins, he is faithful and just to forgive us our sins, and to cleanse us from all unrighteousness." I John 1:9

I am a debtor because of Christ!

"Therefore, brethren, we are debtors, not to the flesh, to live after the flesh."

Romans 8:12

I am reconciled by His Blood!

"And, having made peace through the blood of his cross, by him to reconcile all things unto himself; by him, I say, whether they be things in earth, or things in heaven." Colossians 1:20

"Much more then, being now justified by his blood, we shall be saved from wrath through him." Romans 5:9

"Neither by the blood of goats and calves, but by his own blood he entered in once into the holy place, having obtained eternal redemption for us." Hebrews 9:12

I am entrusted with the gospel!

"But as we were allowed of God to be put in trust with the gospel, even so we speak; not as pleasing men, but God, which trieth our hearts." I Thessalonians 2:4

I am a steward!

"Let a man so account of us, as of the ministers of Christ, and stewards of the mysteries of God." I Corinthians 4:1

I am chosen!

"Ye have not chosen me, but I have chosen you, and ordained you, that ye should go and bring forth fruit, and that your fruit should remain: that whatsoever ye shall ask of the Father in my name, he may give it you." John 15:16

I am awake!

"Wherefore he saith, Awake thou that sleepest, and arise from the dead, and Christ shall give thee light. See then that ye walk circumspectly, not as fools, but as wise, Redeeming the time, because the days are evil." Ephesians 5:14-16

I am never tempted by the Lord!

"Let no man say when he is tempted, I am tempted of God: for God cannot be tempted with evil, neither tempteth he any man:" James 1:13

I am to set my affections on things above!

"If ye then be risen with Christ, seek those things which are above, where Christ sitteth on the right hand of God. Set your affection on things above, not on things on the earth. For ye are dead, and your life is hid with Christ in God." Colossians 3:1-3

I am to occupy until He comes back!

"And he called his ten servants— and said, Occupy till I come." Luke 19:13

I am taught of God!

"But as touching brotherly love ye need not that I write unto you: for ye yourselves are taught of God to love one another." I Thessalonians 4:9

I am honest toward them that are without (outside the grace of God)!

"And that ye study to be quiet, and to do your own business, and to work with your own hands, as we commanded you; That ye may walk honestly toward them that are without, and that ye may have lack of nothing." I Thessalonians 4:11, 12

I am waiting for the Lord!

"Lead me in thy truth, and teach me: for thou art the God of my salvation; on thee do I wait all the day." Psalm 25:5

"And to wait for his Son from heaven, whom he raised from the dead, even Jesus, which delivered us from the wrath to come." I Thessalonians 1:10

"Wait on the Lord: be of good courage, and he shall strengthen thine heart: wait, I say, on the Lord." Psalm 27:14

I am beloved!

"To the praise of the glory of his grace, wherein he hath made us accepted in the beloved." Ephesians 1:6

"But ye, beloved, building up yourselves on your most holy faith, praying in the Holy Ghost," Jude 20

I am a follower!

"My soul followeth hard after thee: thy right hand upholdeth me." Psalm 63:8

I am not afraid!

"But he saith unto them, it is I; be not afraid." John 6:20

I am doing unto the Lord!

"And whatsoever ye do in word or deed, do all in the name of the Lord Jesus, giving thanks to God and the Father by him. And whatsoever ye do, do it heartily, as to the Lord, and not unto men; Knowing that of the Lord ye shall receive the reward of the inheritance: for ye serve the Lord Christ." Colossians 3:17, 23, 24

I am sent!

"And Jesus came and spake unto them, saying, All power is given unto me in heaven and in earth. Go ye therefore, and teach all nations, baptizing them in the name of the Father, and of the Son, and of the Holy Ghost: Teaching them to observe all things whatsoever I have commanded you: and, lo, I am with you alway, even unto the end of the world. Amen." Matthew 28:18-20

I am working together with Him!

"We then, as workers together with him, beseech you also that ye receive not the grace of God in vain." II Corinthians 6:1

I am called unto His kingdom!

"That ye would walk worthy of God, who hath called you unto his kingdom and glory."
I Thessalonians 2:12

I am trusted to stay awake (be counted on at all times)!

"And that, knowing the time, that now it is high time to awake out of sleep: for now is our salvation nearer than when we believed." Romans 13: 11

I am redeeming the time I have with others!

"Walk in wisdom toward them that are without, redeeming the time." Colossians 4:5

I am entrusted with eternal life!

"That whosoever believeth in him should not perish, but have eternal life." John 3:15

"Whereof I am made a minister, according to the dispensation of God which is given to me for you, to fulfil the word of God;" Colossians 1:25

"For if I do this thing willingly, I have a reward: but if against my will, a dispensation of the gospel is committed unto me." I Corinthians 9:17

I am not alienated!

"This say therefore, and testify in the Lord, that ye henceforth walk not as other Gentiles walk, in the vanity of their mind, Having the understanding darkened, being alienated from the life of God through the ignorance that is in them, because of the blindness of their heart:" Ephesians 4:17,18

Victory

I am a king and priest unto God the Father!

"And hath made us kings and priests unto God and his Father; to him be glory and dominion for ever and ever. Amen." Revelation 1:6

"And hast made us unto our God kings and priests: and we shall reign on the earth." Revelation 5:10

I am coming back when He comes back!

"And I saw heaven opened, and behold a white horse; and he that sat upon him was called Faithful and True, and in righteousness he doth judge and make war. His eyes were as a flame of fire, and on his head were many crowns; and he had a name written, that no man knew, but he himself. And he was clothed with a vesture dipped in blood: and his name is called The Word of God. And the armies which were in heaven followed him upon white horses, clothed in fine linen, white and clean." Revelation 19:11-14

I am to reign in life!

"For if by one man's offence death reigned by one; much more they which receive abundance of grace and of the gift of righteousness shall reign in life by one, Jesus Christ.)" Romans 5:17

I am entrusted with suffering!

"For I reckon that the sufferings of this present time are not worthy to be compared with the glory which shall be revealed in us." Romans 8:18

I am quickened by His Spirit!

"But if the Spirit of him that raised up Jesus from the dead dwell in you, he that raised up Christ from the dead shall also quicken your mortal bodies by his Spirit that dwelleth in you." Romans 8:11

I am called!

"Moreover whom he did predestinate, them he also called: and whom he called, them he also justified: and whom he justified, them he also glorified." Romans 8:30

I am free from the world, the flesh, and the devil!

"Knowing this, that our old man is crucified with him, that the body of sin might be destroyed, that henceforth we should not serve sin." Romans 6:6

"I am crucified with Christ: nevertheless I live; yet not I, but Christ liveth in me: and the life which I now live in the flesh I live by the faith of the Son of God, who loved me, and gave himself for me." Galatians 2:20

"And they that are Christ's have crucified the flesh with the affections and lusts." Galatians 5:24

I am His workmanship!

"For we are his workmanship, created in Christ Jesus unto good works, which God hath before ordained that we should walk in them." Ephesians 2:10

I am saved!

"For God sent not his Son into the world to condemn the world; but that the world through him might be saved." John 3:17

"And it shall come to pass, that whosoever shall call on the name of the Lord shall be saved." Acts 2:21

"Neither is there salvation in any other: for there is none other name under heaven given among men, whereby we must be saved." Acts 4:12

"And they said, Believe on the Lord Jesus Christ, and thou shalt be saved, and thy house." Acts 16:31

"For whosoever shall call upon the name of the Lord shall be saved." Romans 10:13

I am Born Again by the Blood of Christ!

"But now in Christ Jesus ye who sometimes were far off are made nigh by the blood of Christ." Ephesians 2:13

"Being born again, not of corruptible seed, but of incorruptible, by the word of God, which liveth and abideth forever." I Peter 1:23

I am being saved!

"Who delivered us from so great a death, and doth deliver: in whom we trust that he will yet deliver us;" II Corinthians 1; 10

I am free from condemnation!

"There is therefore now no condemnation to them which are in Christ Jesus, who walk not after the flesh, but after the Spirit. For the law of the Spirit of life in Christ Jesus hath made me free from the law of sin and death. For what the law could not do, in that it was weak through the flesh, God sending his own Son in the likeness of sinful flesh, and for sin, condemned sin in the flesh: That the righteousness of the law might be fulfilled in us, who walk not after the flesh, but after the Spirit." Romans 8:1-4

I am clothed in the armor of light!

"The night is far spent, the day is at hand: let us therefore cast off the works of darkness, and let us put on the armour of light." Romans 13; 12

"But if we walk in the light, as he is in the light, we have fellowship one with another, and the blood of Jesus Christ his Son cleanseth us from all sin." I John 1:7

I am strong in Christ!

"Finally, my brethren, be strong in the Lord, and the power of his might." Ephesians 6:10

"Therefore I take pleasure in infirmities, in reproaches, in necessities, in persecutions, in distresses for Christ's sake: for when I am weak, then am I strong." II Corinthians 12:10

I am free from the curse!

"Christ hath redeemed us from the curse of the law, being made a curse for us: for it is written, Cursed is every one that hangeth on a tree:" Galatians 3:13

I am - while yet a sinner!

"But God commendeth his love toward us, in that, while we were yet sinners, Christ died for us." Romans 5:8

"According as he hath chosen us in him before the foundation of the world, that we should be holy and without blame before him in love:" Ephesians 1:4

"The eyes of your understanding being enlightened; that ye may know what is the hope of his calling, and what the riches of the glory of his inheritance in the saints, And what is the exceeding greatness of his power to us-ward who believe, according to the working of his mighty power, Which he wrought in Christ, when he raised him from the dead, and set him at his own right hand in the heavenly places," Ephesians 1:18-20

I am triumphing in the Cross!

"And having spoiled principalities and powers, he made a show of them openly, triumphing over them in it." Colossians 2:15

I am meet (fit) to be a partaker!

"Giving thanks unto the Father, which hath made us meet to be partakers of the inheritance of the saints in light:" Colossians 1:12

I am an overcomer!

"These things I have spoken unto you, that in me ye might have peace. In the world ye shall have tribulation: but be of good cheer; I have overcome the world." John 16:33

I am the victor because of Jesus Christ!

"But thanks be to God, which giveth us the victory through our Lord Jesus Christ." I Corinthians 15:57

I am constrained!

"For the love of Christ constraineth us; because we thus judge, that if one died for all, then were all dead: And that he died for all, that they which live should not henceforth live unto themselves, but unto him which died for them, and rose again."

II Corinthians 5:14

I am not in the flesh!

"But ye are not in the flesh, but in the Spirit, if so be that the Spirit of God dwell in you. Now if any man have not the Spirit of Christ, he is none of his." Romans 8:9

"This I say then, Walk in the Spirit, and ye shall not fulfil the lust of the flesh."

Galatians 5; 16

I am reconciled!

"And you, that were sometime alienated and enemies in your mind by wicked works, yet now hath he reconciled" Colossians 1:21

"For if, when we were enemies, we were reconciled to God by the death of his Son, much more, being reconciled, we shall be saved by his life." Romans 5:10

Death

I am delivered from the fear of death!

"Forasmuch then as the children are partakers of flesh and blood, he also himself likewise took part of the same; that through death he might destroy him that had the power of death, that is, the devil; And deliver them who through fear of death were all their lifetime subject to bondage." Hebrews 2:14, 15

I am delivered from this present evil world!

"Who gave himself for our sins, that he might deliver us from this present evil world, according to the will of God and our Father:" Galatians 1:4

I am blessed!

"Blessed and holy is he that hath part in the first resurrection: on such the second death hath no power, but they shall be priests of God and of Christ, and shall reign with him a thousand years." Revelation 20:6

"And there shall be no night there; and they need no candle, neither light of the sun; for the Lord God giveth them light: and they shall reign for ever and ever." Revelation 22:5

I am dead from the rudiments of the world!

"Wherefore if ye be dead with Christ from the rudiments of the world, why, as though living in the world, are ye subject to ordinances, (Touch not; taste not; handle not; Which all are to perish with the using;) after the commandments and doctrines of men?" Colossians 2:20-22

NOTES

NOTES

Jesus said,

"Be ye therefore ready also: For the Son of man cometh at an hour when ye think not. " Luke 12:40

Are you ready?

The Promise of His coming!

"And if I go and prepare a place for you, I will come again, and receive you unto myself; that where I am, there ye may be also." John 14:3

"…Ye men of Galilee, why stand ye gazing up into heaven? this same Jesus, which is taken up from you into heaven, shall so come in like manner as ye have seen him go into heaven." Acts 1:11

"For the Lord himself shall descend from heaven with a shout, with the voice of the archangel, and with the trump of God…" I Thessalonians 4:16

The Penalty for failure to be ready at His coming!

"And these shall go away into everlasting punishment…" Matthew 25:46a

"For the wages of sin is death…" Romans 6:23a

"And whosoever was not found written in the book of life was cast into the lake of fire." Revelation 20:15

"How shall we escape, if we neglect so great salvation…" Hebrews 2:3a

The Preparation for His coming!

All Have Sinned

"For all have sinned, and come short of the glory of God;" Romans 3:23

"All we like sheep have gone astray; we have turned everyone to his own way; and the Lord hath laid on him the iniquity of us all." Isaiah 53:6

Jesus Paid Your Sin Debt

"But God commendeth his love toward us, in that, while we were yet sinners, Christ died for us." Romans 5:8

"Who his own self bare our sins in his own body on the tree…" I Peter 2:24a

Repent (turn from your sins)

"I tell you, Nay: but, except ye repent, ye shall all likewise perish." Luke 13:3

Call on the Lord

"For whosoever shall call upon the name of the Lord shall be saved." Romans 10:13

Pray – Dear Lord, I confess that I am a sinner. I turn from my sins to You; please forgive me and come into my life. **I believe that Jesus died, was buried, and rose again the third day from the dead for me.**

Take control of my life and make me the kind of person You want me to be.

Thank You for hearing my prayer and coming into my life as You promised. Amen.

If you would like more information on the Christian life, you may contact Dale Vick through the Rock Ministries at **www.HeistheRock.org**

Dale E. Vick

Notes

www.ingramcontent.com/pod-product-compliance
Lightning Source LLC
Chambersburg PA
CBHW080010050426
42446CB00036B/3332